COOL CAREERS WITHOUT COLLEGE

CAREERS FOR PEOPLE WHO LOVE COOKING

Morgan Williams

T0246500

ROSEN
PUBLISHING

Published in 2021 by The Rosen Publishing Group, Inc.
29 East 21st Street, New York, NY 10010

Copyright © 2021 by The Rosen Publishing Group, Inc.

First Edition

Portions of this work were originally authored by Sarah Machajewski and
published as *Cool Careers Without College for People Who Love to Cook &
Eat*. All new material in this edition authored by Morgan Williams.

Library of Congress Cataloging-in-Publication Data

Names: Williams, Morgan, author.
Title: Careers for people who love cooking / Morgan Williams.
Description: New York : Rosen Publishing, [2021]
| Series: Cool careers without college
Identifiers: LCCN 2019059539 | ISBN 9781499468748 (library binding) | ISBN
    9781499468731 (paperback)
Subjects: LCSH: Cooking—Vocational guidance—Juvenile literature. | Food
    service—Vocational guidance—Juvenile literature.
Classification: LCC TX652.5 .W55187 2020 | DDC 647.95023—dc23
LC record available at https://lccn.loc.gov/2019059539

Some of the images in this book illustrate individuals who are
models. The depictions do not imply actual situations or events.

Manufactured in the United States of America

Find us on

CONTENTS

INTRODUCTION

There are few things that bring people together like preparing and eating food. No matter what kind of food is preferred—from pizza to tacos to hamburgers to grilled veggies—everyone likes to gather with friends and family to get their grub on. It's not just the act of eating together that creates strong bonds between people—it's also the act of cooking. Taking a few or many different ingredients and combining them in different ways provides a unique sense of satisfaction and joy to those people we call cooks or chefs.

If you've thought about all these things already, you may have the soul of a cook inside you. Those who have made it big in the world of food often had their passions for the kitchen awoken at a young age. Being deeply connected to food preparation is a must for anyone who wants to have a successful, rewarding career in the field. It's a path suited to those who truly love experimenting, learning on the fly, and most of all, eating. For those with an undeniable connection to the kitchen, there are countless opportunities—even without an advanced degree and years of formal study.

There are also many job prospects for people who simply love restaurants and the food industry in general, not just for those who want to actually prepare food. Though celebrity chefs get the most attention, their success is directly related to the quality of the staff around them—and, as in any field, good help is hard to find. Though some on-the-job training is necessary for entry-level and intermediate food-related positions, there is a global community of cooks, chefs, and restaurateurs who will welcome you with open arms. With nothing but a high school diploma, a dedication to the craft, and a committed desire to learn and improve, you can become a member of the fast-paced and dynamic food and restaurant industry.

CHAPTER 1

STAFFING THE RESTAURANT

Because the food industry is so broad, there are many different places at which a curious young person can jump in. Perhaps the easiest is with an entry-level position at a local or chain restaurant. Generally, this means taking a job as a host or a server. While nearly everyone knows what these people do, not everyone understands how tough—but rewarding—it can be.

Hosts and hostesses are responsible for keeping things running smoothly in what is called the front of the house, or the part of the restaurant where customers eat and drink. While the head chef keeps things moving in the kitchen, the host helps run things in the front. This starts with seating customers, distributing menus, and assigning tables to servers. Though they're rarely involved with food, starting as a host is a great first step toward becoming a server.

Being a server—also called a waiter or waitress—requires a combination of knowledge about customer service, food preparation, and business interactions. More than just the people who bring you your food, servers provide suggestions and deal with customers' problems—they are the lifeblood of any successful restaurant.

Restaurant waitstaff are responsible for connecting customers to the kitchen.

SERVE AND SMILE

Food servers are the link between a restaurant's customers and the kitchen. As soon as customers are seated, their server influences a lot of their experience. One of the most important parts of gaining and keeping a serving job is the ability to provide "service with a smile." Customer service is how you treat and interact with customers. Providing excellent customer service means going the extra mile to accommodate customers' requests and needs. Most servers will tell you that good customer service is all about being polite, friendly, and, most importantly, patient. Because customers interact with servers more than anyone else in a restaurant, these qualities—or the lack thereof—can greatly impact the restaurant's reputation, no matter how good the food is.

Servers are expected to take orders, serve food, and set and clear tables. Crucially, servers must also communicate messages between customers and the kitchen. Successful servers make themselves familiar with the menu and how each item is prepared. This helps in answering customer questions and giving them advice on food they may enjoy. For example, a server can warn customers with allergies against ordering certain dishes, or tell the kitchen to alter menu items for customers with dietary restrictions. Depending on the restaurant, they may be required to know even more. Servers in ethnic restaurants may have to interpret the menu for diners who are

If you find a job at a high-end restaurant, expect to take on more responsibilities during each shift than you would at a more casual establishment.

THE BASICS OF FINE DINING

Many servers aspire to hold a job in a high-end restaurant. It can be a lucrative gig: the money is better than at other restaurants, the environment is more luxurious, and you'll likely be working with some of the highest-quality food around. However, excelling as a fine-dining server is no easy task. Some of the etiquette for these upscale environments that servers must follow includes:

- **Welcoming guests.** Servers first introduce themselves to their guests, letting the customers know they will be taking care of them for the evening. They provide menus and a thorough explanation of the night's specials.
- **Establishing rapport.** It's a good idea for servers to make light conversation with their tables. This makes the diners feel comfortable and welcomed, which can lead to a better dining experience and more generous tips. A conversation starter could be asking if the table is out for a special occasion or what they're looking forward to having. Servers must be careful not to overstep their boundaries, though. Being too chatty can be annoying to some diners, especially at luxury establishments.
- **Serving the meal.** Formal fine-dining etiquette states that service starts on the right and moves in a clockwise direction around the table. The exception is if the food is being served family style, in which case service goes to the left. A general rule of thumb is that women are served before men. Further, at special events like weddings, the guests of honor are served first, regardless of their position.

- **Keeping a neat table.** Servers are expected to clear the table between courses—and all at once. Seasoned servers know not to remove plates or glasses from one diner while another is still eating, which can be interpreted as the meal being rushed. Servers will also clear the table of crumbs or even replace a tablecloth if it appears to be dirty. Cleanliness is highly important to most high-end diners.

- **Presenting the bill.** Handling the check can sometimes create an awkward situation for diners and servers alike. Servers always present the check after the meal, dessert, and after-dinner drinks are finished—never before. In fine-dining situations, the presentation of the bill must be discreet and respectful, as guests most likely don't wish to discuss the payment.

Knowing when and how to clear plates in between courses is a vital part of a server's job at an upscale restaurant.

unfamiliar with the cuisine. In some restaurants, a food server may be asked to recommend the best wines to complement a meal or even perform some food preparation at customers' tables. That guacamole isn't going to make itself!

Serving jobs are available in several different environments. Where you choose to work depends on where you'd be most comfortable. Coffee shop employees, for example, must be fast and efficient, since their customers are in a hurry. Being able to work under pressure is a necessary skill. On the other side of the spectrum, high-end restaurants offer a more leisurely dining experience. Customers at these kinds of restaurants expect impeccable and knowledgeable service from servers who won't rush them. There are also many styles of restaurants between these two extremes.

Many people choose to wait tables because the flexible schedule gives them time to pursue other interests. Servers are sometimes students who need part-time work, parents who have other responsibilities, or people in creative and competitive fields, such as acting, who need a steady income. A serving job is flexible enough that you can make money while still dedicating a lot of time elsewhere. The drawback is that people who wait tables often don't have a consistent weekly schedule. Shifts may change or be called off without warning. In addition, food servers know that they may be asked to work very early or very late, even if they aren't regularly scheduled to do so.

It's also worth considering the physical demands of the job. Servers are always on their feet and spend a lot of time walking back and forth between tables and the kitchen, often with heavy trays of food and drinks. If you have back problems or get tired easily, this career is not the best choice for you.

Based on what you've read so far, you probably know if a serving job fits your personality. A word of warning, though: if you have trouble dealing with people, this is definitely not the job for you. No matter how many times you have to clean up a spill or how rude a particular customer may be, your job depends on the "three Cs"—being cool, calm, and collected.

DO YOU HAVE WHAT IT TAKES?

Because they are entry-level positions, serving jobs rarely require formal education or training. This makes them a great option for teens who are still in high school or for anybody who wants to see if the food industry is the right fit for them in general. A big part of getting hired to a restaurant's waitstaff is the ability to learn as you go—quickly. Many restaurants have a brief orientation to help servers become comfortable with the specifics of their operations, but they expect new employees to learn the ropes quickly. New hires are often assigned to shadow experienced servers within their first few days on the job.

A person's first serving gig is unlikely to be at a high-end restaurant. These establishments require a good deal of experience because customers expect a certain level of service. Waitstaff at the fanciest restaurants must perform the basics perfectly before they can perform more complicated tasks—which they must also learn to perfect.

Your best bet is to start off with a part-time job as a server while you're in school. Many local and chain restaurants can accommodate school schedules and are willing to provide training. Holding a part-time

Waiting tables is typically a fast-paced job—and you'll have to learn as you go if you want to succeed.

serving job, even if it's just over the summer, is a valuable experience for those interested in a culinary career. It gives you a great advantage later on, even if you decide to pursue other roles in the food industry.

THE FUTURE OF WAITSTAFF

You've probably heard about the minimum wage. If you want to be a server, however, you can forget it! In most restaurants, waiters and waitresses have a base salary that is far below the national or statewide minimum wage. It's often just a few dollars per hour. The real moneymaking opportunity is found in the tips. Most customers know that servers depend on tips. In the United States, it's customary for servers to receive around 20 percent of the final bill as their tip.

Restaurants that have a wealthier clientele and more expensive menus may pay a higher hourly wage. What's more, fine-dining servers can expect to make good tips because the food and drinks are typically far more expensive in these kinds of establishments. Be aware, though, that servers are sometimes expected to split their tips with the rest of the house. At the end of the night, servers give some of their tips to the hosts, bartenders, and bussers who aided them in serving their tables.

While the majority of waitstaff jobs—especially at smaller chains or local restaurants—don't provide medical or retirement benefits, they may offer different perks, such as free or discounted meals. Some restaurants also provide uniforms for their employees.

According to the 2018 edition of the Bureau of Labor Statistics's *Occupational Outlook Handbook*, the future looks good for waiters and waitresses, with an expected 6 percent growth between 2018 and 2028. Waitstaff jobs are usually plentiful, as restaurants are always opening or expanding. Additionally, due to the high turnover rate in the field, many restaurants hire new employees constantly. Most cities and towns have many different kinds of eating establishments, so the field is wide open for a young person who is eager to learn the ins and outs of restaurant work. What's more, as more and more people go out to eat, restaurants are growing and hiring bigger staffs to accommodate the increase in business. All this adds up to increased, and better, opportunities for entry-level servers.

CHAPTER 2

FOOD MANAGEMENT 101

When you think of a restaurant, the first thing that comes to mind is probably all the delicious food it might serve. However, running an eating establishment is a complex business. There are customers to keep happy, servers and hosts to pay, and menus to prepare. Of course, there's also money to be made. Enter the restaurant manager, whose job is to maintain the delicate balancing act that is required to operate an eatery.

Unlike servers and hosts, whose daily tasks are often clearly defined, a restaurant manager's responsibilities can change from day to day. First and foremost, they must be informed about everything that occurs in the establishment. From restocking inventory to acquiring new cooks to addressing customer complaints, the manager is involved every step of the way, either directly or indirectly. When there is too much work for the manager alone to handle, they must be able to delegate tasks to other trusted staff members.

Mastering all these skills is far from easy, and there are few people who are capable of competently supervising an entire restaurant. If you enjoy the idea of working at the meeting point of customer service, food preparation, human resources, and business sense, then a career as a restaurant manager may be for you.

Restaurant managers must be able to keep the restaurant's service efficient and friendly.

WORKING YOUR WAY UP

Managing a restaurant requires organizational skills, a solid understanding of basic business principles, and a thorough understanding of how the food service industry operates. The most important of a restaurant manager's responsibilities is ensuring smooth coordination between the floor staff and the kitchen staff.

Most managers start in entry-level service positions—as servers, hosts, or bussers—and work their way up over time. Though this process can seem slow at times, there are many benefits from starting at the bottom. One such benefit is that an experienced manager will be aware of the general working conditions for the people they manage. They can implement changes they know will have a positive impact and make people happy.

At the same time, the role of running a restaurant separates the manager from the rest of the employees. Staff members have to view the manager as a supervisor, rather than a coworker. Moreover, managing others includes responsibilities that can be unpleasant. For example, a restaurant manager may have to fire people who can't obey basic rules, such as showing up on time, or worse, employees who are stealing from the business.

In addition to these basic managerial tasks, restaurant managers also need to know a lot about food. Although managers don't often directly prepare the food (though they may help in a pinch), they

Managers work closely with their staff members to make sure the restaurant is well supplied each week.

usually choose suppliers and approve of and order ingredients. Of course, all this purchasing must be done within a budget, which the manager may help plan. Further, the manager may work with chefs and cooks to come up with creative ideas, such as seasonal menu items and promotions. All of these things help the restaurant turn a profit.

Be prepared to work a lot of hours if you choose to be a restaurant manager. While it's an undeniably interesting and often fun job, you may be called upon to handle unplanned crises. If the ice machine breaks or if a pipe in the men's restroom bursts, you can't abandon the restaurant—even if your shift is almost over. Managing a restaurant can be highly stressful, as customer complaints and employee issues are often passed along to the person in charge: you. As with a food server, patience is key in this role. Quickly addressing both customer concerns and staff conflicts is necessary for a business's survival.

As a restaurant manager, you must go into the job knowing that it's a lot of work. You are responsible for everything that goes on in the restaurant, so if work isn't accomplished, you are ultimately to blame. It takes exceptional interpersonal skills to know how to effectively delegate tasks and see them through to completion. To help with this, good managers try to create a strong team environment. If employees feel that their manager supports and encourages them, they'll be more willing to do a good job.

WHAT MAKES A MANAGER?

Many managers can trace their roots in the industry back to entry-level positions, beginning their careers as cooks, hosts, bartenders, or food servers. Of course, to move above these roles, every manager has mastered many aspects of running a restaurant. Previous experience in the field is important because it gives managers a better understanding of restaurant employees and some general skills in the business. The average restaurant manager has spent three or

DAY AND NIGHT DIFFERENCES

Restaurants are open at all different times of the day. Some establishments are open only for dinner, some places only do breakfast, and others are open for 24 hours. If a restaurant is open for more than one meal, it will usually employ more than one manager to cover its hours of operation. One will cover the opening of the restaurant, and the other will cover the closing. The opening shift is very different from the closing shift, and managers' duties and responsibilities vary significantly based on which one they cover.

As an opening manager, one must be prepared to get there early. This shift is dedicated to one thing and one thing only: making sure the restaurant is ready to open on time. Managers and other restaurant staff use the few short hours before customers are allowed in to get both the food and the space ready for customers. This can involve chopping produce or preparing large quantities of menu items that aren't made to order. Opening managers (sometimes referred to as "morning" or "day" managers) may also get the dining area of the restaurant ready by setting tables and stocking items such as napkins and condiments. Ultimately, the managers are there to make sure that everything goes off without a hitch and that the restaurant is fully prepared to take on the day's customers.

Closing managers have quite the daunting job: they oversee all aspects of shutting the restaurant down. Can you imagine how much there is to do? Closing managers make sure that the restaurant is thoroughly cleaned, the floors are mopped or vacuumed, and the garbage is taken out. They also make sure that food is properly stored and that nothing is left out to spoil or become contaminated. Some restaurants also use the closing shift to prepare food for the next day. This can involve anything from slicing lemons to baking bread. Closing managers have one more very important job: counting the day's earnings. This is a lot of responsibility, and it's usually reserved for the most trusted of managers.

The closing shift at a restaurant can be tough, but managers must be sure that everything gets done so the next day can start strong.

four years in the trenches, gaining all the knowledge needed to supervise an establishment successfully.

A college degree is not necessary for obtaining a restaurant manager's job. Restaurant owners are more likely to hire someone without a degree who has been in the business for a long time versus someone with a degree but no experience. Just as in many fields, a proven track record in the restaurant business is an important addition to a manager's résumé.

MANAGEMENT: MOVING FORWARD

Most entry-level restaurant positions pay an hourly wage, which means that employees clock in and out and are compensated according to the amount of time spent on the job. In contrast, many restaurant managers earn a salary. This means they are guaranteed a specific yearly amount, which is then divided into smaller paychecks. Salaries are determined by the city in which one works since the cost of living can vary wildly. A manager's salary can also depend on how long they've been with the business, the exact nature of their responsibilities, and how much time they regularly spend at the restaurant. As a manager's responsibilities grow, it's possible to negotiate a higher salary to match the job duties.

Management opportunities are plentiful for people in the food industry who decide to stick it out, if only because of the high turnover rate at lower-level jobs. According to the Bureau of Labor Statistics, restaurant management opportunities are growing rapidly, with a projected 11 percent rise between 2018 and 2028. People who work at a restaurant (or several restaurants) in varying roles are highly likely to become managers after they have put in enough hard work. If you think this career sounds interesting, give it a try—but remember to be patient. The longer you work for a restaurant, the better equipped you'll be to take on a managerial role, should it become available.

CHAPTER 3

COOKING ON THE LINE

Let's be honest: a lot of the action in the food industry is in the cooking. Maybe you like to cook at home, for friends and family—maybe you're good at it, and maybe you enjoy it. If that sounds like you, a career as a cook is a good option. It's important to note that a cook (sometimes called a line cook) is not the same as a chef. In general, a cook is responsible for working with predetermined ingredients to prepare the food from an established menu to serve daily customers at a restaurant.

Most chain and local restaurants—from diners to fast-food establishments—employ cooks to work in the kitchen and execute the owner's vision of the menu. The workspace where food is cooked is called a line, hence the term "line cook." Though people in this job are rarely responsible for coming up with creative new menu items or experimenting with food, there's still a lot of passion involved with being a good cook.

Though line cooks don't have much creative freedom, there is still a lot of satisfaction in getting paid to prepare food every day.

WALK THE LINE

The biggest difference between a chef and a cook is that chefs plan their own menus and concoct their own recipes, while cooks are given menus and recipes to follow. It's a general rule that cooks aren't allowed to stray from the menu or recipes provided by the restaurant. The reasons for this are varied, but it mostly comes down to consistency. This is especially true in chain restaurants and fast-food joints, where dishes have to exactly match what the corporate owner has determined them to be. This helps fulfill customer expectations and maintain the business's brand and identity.

A cook's main responsibility is to prepare food on an as-needed basis, filling orders as they are delivered by the waitstaff. Nowadays, most food is made to order, so cooks have to be efficient and practiced in preparing a meal in which all components of the dish are hot, tasty, and ready to go at the same time. This gets even more complicated when there are multiple orders per table. Not all menu items are made to order, though. Some foods, such as stews, soups, and sauces, can be prepared in advance, making a cook's life easier. They're often made in bulk at the start of the day or shift and are ready to go as they are requested.

If you think about the qualities that make a successful cook, one of the first that should pop into your mind is cleanliness. A cook must always be conscious of maintaining a clean workspace. Because

A clean kitchen helps promote food safety, which is the most important part of any cook's job.

they directly handle the food that people will eat and enjoy, cooks must be aware of food storage regulations and how to prevent cross-contamination of food. For example, some dishes cannot be served with the utensils used to prepare the raw ingredients. An absentminded cook may purposefully prepare a dish with no peanuts for a customer with an allergy but use equipment that came into contact with peanuts earlier to put it on the plate. Doing this could make someone very sick. Food safety is serious business, and it takes a dedicated cook to remember to apply every health and sanitation guideline to each dish they prepare.

NOT A "COOK"IE-CUTTER JOB

Just as there are many varieties of restaurants, there are many kinds of cooks. They all handle something different in the kitchen. Cooks gets their names from the various stations they are in charge of. It can get pretty crowded in there, so knowing who the various cooks are and what they do will make your first day on the job a little less intimidating. A typical restaurant may include:

• **A line cook.** This is the general term for anybody who prepares meals in a kitchen who isn't a chef. Line cooks are also known as *chefs de partie*.

• **A sauté cook.** Taken from French, "to sauté" means "to quickly cook in a pan with fat," and sauté cooks do just that. You'll often see them turning vegetables quickly in the pan to ensure they are cooked evenly. These cooks prepare meat as well as vegetables and the sauces they are served with.

• **A fry cook.** Fry cooks are often thought of as fast-food workers who flip burgers and drop french fries in the fryer, but there are fry cooks in other kinds of kitchens as well. They generally take care of any fried food that comes out of the kitchen.

• **A grill cook.** These cooks work with meat and usually come to the job with some training in the art of grilling. They give grilled steak, chicken, fish, and other proteins the delicious chargrilled flavor that people love.

• **A cold foods cook.** Cold foods cooks take care of anything fresh and crisp. This includes prepping salads, cold sandwiches, fruit side dishes, and other dishes that don't require an oven or a stove.

Grilling is one of the best-known cooking techniques, and grill cooks are masters at cooking this way.

There are several different kinds of cooks. Short-order cooks fill orders as they come in. Their counterpart is the institutional cook. Institutional cooks have a very similar job, but they prepare huge volumes of food. Think about all of the people in hospitals, schools, and office buildings. All of these places have dozens—maybe even hundreds—of employees and visitors who eat at roughly the same time once or twice a day. That's a lot of meals! Most institutional cooks have assistants or work in teams to complete their tasks quickly.

A cook's job can be physically demanding, so keep that in mind if you pursue this career. Not only are cooks on their feet for most of the day, they are often working in hot kitchens, even during the summer. Sometimes, cooks may have to lift large bags of ingredients—like a 50-pound (23 kg) sack of potatoes—and must move around quickly and frequently to make room for people coming in and out of the kitchen.

COOKING QUALIFICATIONS

You may be surprised to learn that most cooking positions require only that a candidate have a high school diploma. College isn't necessary—but hands-on experience in the kitchen is very important. It would be wise to apply only if you have some basic cooking techniques under your belt. Even if you're a whiz at whipping up chicken cordon bleu at home, it's unlikely that you will be able to walk into your first job and nab the head cook position. Preparing food in a professional setting is far different from making dinner for your family at home.

If you want to make it as a cook, your best bet is to seek a part-time job as a line cook or short-order cook while still in school. By the time you finish high school, you'll have a year or two of experience in a professional kitchen. This will help you immensely if you want to move up at your job or seek employment elsewhere.

COOKING UP A PAYCHECK

Just as with restaurant managers, the area in which one lives, the kind of restaurant, and the size of the restaurant are all factors that affect a cook's salary. Most cooks will tell you, too, that the amount of business a restaurant brings in influences salaries as well.

Experience is an important aspect of making money as a cook. The lowest-level cooks will naturally be paid the least, but after a couple of

If you can stick with the same restaurant for many years, you can work your way up to taking on more responsibility.

years, a cook's seniority in the kitchen will lead to more responsibility. In most situations, more responsibility translates to greater compensation.

With the amount and diversity of restaurants out there, you should have no problem finding a job as a cook, as long as you're willing to learn the restaurant's recipes and follow its way of doing things. The Bureau of Labor Statistics reports that, as with restaurant manager positions, cook positions are expected to grow by 11 percent between 2018 and 2028, meaning there will continue to be a lot of opportunities to get in the kitchen.

Like other positions at restaurants, cook positions usually have a high degree of turnover, so that is one thing you'll have on your side as you seek employment. Someone who can consistently keep a cool head in the kitchen over many years will be a valuable asset in any restaurant. Keep in mind, though, that if business slows in an area, it may be necessary to move somewhere with more customers.

CHAPTER 4

IS A CHEF'S COAT WHAT YOU WANT?

Those who can skillfully prepare food have always been considered special people, but with the rise of celebrity chefs and reality cooking TV shows, being a chef is more glamorous than ever. However, becoming one of these highly respected individuals is also extremely tough. While cooking shows can portray artful cooking as effortless, anyone who has worked in the industry knows the challenging path each famous chef had to walk to achieve success.

It takes more than home cooking skills to become a bona fide chef. Even at a local restaurant in a small town, the head chef is likely a seasoned professional who is bursting with ideas and cooking expertise. Though it's not necessary to have a college education to become a chef, it is also not possible to simply walk into a restaurant and become one. It requires a lot of training, experience, and proven passion. Chefs are often considered artists, using ingredients to paint a picture on the plate. Becoming a successful chef is a lifelong quest of self-improvement and food-based experimentation.

LIVING THE DREAM

It should be obvious that chefs must love food in order to be good at their jobs. Highly developed senses of taste and smell are essential too. Being able to create, alter, blend, and execute subtle flavor profiles is the key to separating yourself from the pack.

Chefs are true artists. They look at basic ingredients and envision completed dishes.

Every chef in the kitchen functions as part of a larger restaurant team, so being able to work well with others is crucial. There are several kinds of chefs, all of whom have the common goal of keeping a kitchen running smoothly while producing high-quality plates of food. A kitchen couldn't function without every chef's contributions. As such, all chefs are expected to be responsible and respectful of both their own tasks and those of their coworkers.

The executive chef, also known as the head chef, is at the top of a kitchen's food chain. A person in this position must be a true leader, as they are at the helm of all of the kitchen's operations. They supervise the entire line of chefs. Believe it or not, executive chefs do little actual cooking—their attention is focused on creating recipes, planning menus, adhering to a budget, taking care of inventory, and overseeing other administrative tasks. In many ways, their role is a combination of the duties of an owner, a restaurant manager, and a short-order cook. Executive chefs are the end of the line as far as responsibility goes. They are accountable for everything that goes into and out of the kitchen. Executive chefs are in the position to receive both blame and praise, and the positive aspects of the job are immensely satisfying and rewarding.

Directly under the executive chef is the sous chef, the executive chef's right-hand man or woman. The sous chef is often responsible for the actual cooking of a meal while the head chef supervises other tasks going on in the kitchen. Some sous chefs take the

An executive chef is the king or queen of their kitchen—there is no greater position for someone who loves to cook.

place of the executive chef if they are away, and some work in an apprentice role, watching and learning on the way to becoming an executive chef themselves.

Next in line is the *saucier*, a title taken from the French word for "sauce cook." Sauciers are the high-

est position of all the station cooks, although they are still beneath the sous chef and the head chef. Their main job is to create sauces, though many are also responsible for preparing soups, stews, and sautéed food. In traditional kitchens, sauciers are almost like chemists, using the five basic sauces of classic cuisine—béchamel, velouté, espagnole, hollandaise, and tomato—in various combinations to concoct hundreds of different new sauces. Every saucier has their own special ingredients and measurements, which make the creations of every saucier unique.

Switching gears (and ingredients), on the other side of the kitchen you'll find someone just as specialized and talented as a saucier: the pastry chef. This chef's area of expertise lies in making desserts— the sweetest course! Pastry chefs usually have chef's training but have chosen to focus on the desserts, breads, and other baked goods that complete a meal. Pastry chefs may be responsible for creating a restaurant's dessert menu and conceptualizing and

Pastry chefs have focused their training on whipping up delicious—and often sweet—treats.

testing new sweets recipes. Most pastry chefs gain experience in cooking savory courses before they choose to focus on desserts.

A garde-manger is in charge of all the cold food that comes off the line. Often considered one of the most demanding jobs in the kitchen, the garde-manger preps dishes such as salads, hors d'oeuvres, and various parts of buffets. An artistic flair is helpful for this job, as garde-mangers may oversee the final plating of the food and may even produce ice carvings for special occasions.

Prep cooks are not involved in the actual cooking of food. Instead, they prepare (as the name implies) the ingredients of the meals on a planned menu. Their assigned tasks can range from peeling potatoes or shrimp to mincing garlic and chopping fresh herbs. Most prep cooks hope to become chefs, and this position is a great stepping-stone because it allows them to develop important talents and techniques, such as knife skills, that are required to become a bona fide chef.

No matter the variety of chef, shifts are often long and challenging. It isn't an easy job. Most chefs work days that last 12 hours or longer, and they must be available for early mornings, late evenings, weekends, and holidays. They are truly dedicated to their craft and work hard to make their creations perfect.

EARNING THE CHEF'S COAT

Like many positions in a restaurant, a career as a chef doesn't strictly require a college degree. However, if you're thinking of becoming a chef, some sort of higher education or formal training is necessary. The quickest way to get on track as a chef is to go to culinary school. There are many schools around the world that offer culinary programs. Culinary schools educate aspiring chefs in the art—and science—of food preparation. Students spend most of their class time in an actual kitchen, gaining hands-on experience with preparing classical dishes and handling common kitchen equipment. Holding a degree from a culinary school shows potential employers that you already know the basics of food preparation and are ready to jump right into the often hectic world of the kitchen.

Education isn't the only thing necessary to become a chef. It's widely understood that there is no true substitute for experience. Many chefs choose to learn the old-fashioned way: they work their way up the ranks by watching and learning from seasoned chefs in working kitchens. This is especially true of entry-level cooks who wish to become executive chefs someday. Everyone starts somewhere before rising to the top!

If you have a talent for cooking but you don't think cooking school is right for you, try your hand working as a line cook in a local restaurant. Another option is to take occasional classes while you work in a restaurant to improve your skills.

A CHEF'S JOB SECURITY

Achieving the title of chef can be both personally and financially satisfying. As with all industries, entry-level positions always pay less than those at the top of the hierarchy. As you get years of experience under your belt, you should find yourself working upward through several different positions while your salary also increases. Additionally, the more specialized your skills are, the more you can attempt to negotiate after a job offer. For example, a chef with a culinary degree, pastry experience, and the proven ability to make sauces will be able to demand more than a new chef who has taken just a few classes.

Ultimately, salaries for chefs vary. Factors in one's salary include restaurant size and location. A chef who cooks for 100 customers a night in a busy city has the opportunity to make a larger income than one who works in a less populated area.

Culinary schools offer aspiring chefs the training they need to get ahead in a competitive industry.

The amount and availability of jobs for chefs is good, and the Bureau of Labor Statistics predicts that positions will remain highly available. Growth for a chef's employment opportunities is an estimated 11 percent between 2018 and 2028. However, it's worth noting that job competition will remain difficult in upscale restaurants and high-end hotels, simply because there is a much greater potential for high pay in these places than in the average restaurant.

Besides working in a traditional restaurant, new chefs have the additional options of heading up cooking lines in hospitals, colleges, hotels, and casinos. Some chefs also decide to take their skills to the classroom and pass them on to a whole new generation of culinary whiz kids by becoming teachers or professors.

Like other food industry positions, there is a substantial amount of turnover among chefs, so the payoff can be great for committed and persistent people who stay in the industry long enough to nab the higher positions. Importantly, continual learning helps chefs build their cooking repertoire and keep their skills fresh and up to date.

CHAPTER 5

CATERING THE BIG EVENT

You may think that all restaurant jobs require you to be stuck inside a busy building day in and day out. Nothing could be further from the truth. One example of a job in food that literally takes you outside the box is catering. You've probably been to a big event—like a wedding or birthday party—at which food was served to the entire group at once. If so, you've seen a caterer at work. Blending the business, food prep, and cooking components of a head chef, a caterer cuts out some aspects of customer service necessary at a restaurant and replaces them with the logistics and organization necessary for transporting food from a kitchen to an event.

FEEDING THE MASSES

Catering, in short, is the business of transporting and serving food at a location far from where it's prepared. Caterers supply food to people who can't or don't

Being a good caterer requires skills both similar to and different from those required for being a traditional cook, especially for large events.

have time to make it themselves. Good caterers take skills and tricks from restaurant chefs, bakers, and food stylists and use them to serve food that is both memorable and pleasing at events for large groups.

People most often seek out catering services when they need food for a large group. "Large" is relative here—it can mean anything from 5 to 5,000 people. As a caterer, you may prepare food for a small office lunch one day and a huge conference the next. The best thing you can do as a caterer is only accept business that is manageable for the size and scale of your operation. One important component of a successfully catered event is having just the right amount of food. Overpreparing will lead to waste and loss of profits, while underpreparing will lead to unhappy customers.

There are many different varieties of catering. Some people choose to cater in their spare time and run small businesses from their homes. There are also large companies (hotels, for instance) that may have dedicated catering teams ready to spring into action. Fast-food and chain restaurants have begun to offer catering as well, and even some grocery stores have gotten in on the action. This is because demand for catering is high.

Caterers are hired for their expertise. Clients may have a general idea of the food they would like at their event but also value the creative menu and display suggestions of a caterer. People skills are an important part of being a successful caterer, but they're not quite the same skills required of a server. Imagine a situation in which a client demands several tweaks to a menu in a short period of time. This is a very different interaction from a customer complaining that their food was wrong at a restaurant! Making them happy while maintaining your culinary integrity requires patience and understanding. Ultimately, if a client and caterer cannot communicate well, it will hurt the overall success of an event—and neither side wants that.

Caterers must be able to work closely with their clients to come up with a menu that fits dietary desires and budgetary restrictions.

Caterers also need to adapt quickly. For instance, if a caterer's usual supplier of vegetables is closed or out of certain ingredients, they cannot simply tell a client that the menu has to be changed on the day of the event. People hire caterers because they expect important functions to go smoothly, professionally, and deliciously. They're paying money so that they don't have to think about supply lines and food preparation.

The type and amount of food that caterers serve can vary. Some clients may request only sandwich fixings for hungry executives at a board meeting. Others may want to serve a five-course traditional French meal. A lot of caterers have professional cooking backgrounds that help them create menus. However, it's not just about the food. Caterers usually remain available at an event, providing dinnerware, setting tables, and tearing it all down at the end of the night. Many also provide waitstaff and bartenders.

No matter the size of the event, organization is key. Less than half of a caterer's work time is actually devoted to cooking. The rest is spent transporting food and hiring personnel. Some caterers rent—instead of own—the majority of the equipment they use, so finding and acquiring special dishes and tools can take a lot of time. If they are serving alcohol at a function, they may need to apply for special licenses or permissions.

Catering can open doors to other interesting lines of work as well. Preparing and providing meals on a large scale can give an aspiring chef ideas for opening their own restaurant or breaking out as a private chef. Some caterers move on to general event planning, which can involve hiring caterers and entertainment, or they may jump to other fields entirely, such as floral supply or equipment rental.

GETTING INTO CATERING

Many culinary schools offer catering classes, but they are not necessary for starting down that path. Many people begin at home, experimenting with various types of cuisine in order to have a strong foundation of different meals from which their clients can choose. Home catering businesses have very low overhead (operating costs), and people can do it part-time to test out the market in their area. If you're thinking about going into catering, another

If you want to start your own business, you'll have to do a lot of groundwork to succeed.

option is to work a few hours a week for a small caterer in the area.

If you do start your own catering enterprise, be as aggressive—and professional—as possible. Hit the pavement and post advertisements. Talk to other businesses that sell supplies for special events, such as flower shops and liquor stores, to see what it takes to obtain clients. Maybe they even have an upcoming event that needs catering. Creating a website or social media page is another great way to get the word out about your services.

Yet another way to investigate the business is to seek employment at a hotel or a banquet facility. These businesses are frequently hosting special affairs, and the experience an aspiring caterer can obtain here is invaluable. As an added bonus, working at established companies doesn't require the initial investment that would be needed to start your own business.

Training for a prospective catering career doesn't have to begin in such a focused manner, however. Any time spent working in a restaurant is extremely helpful, from waiting tables to working as a line cook. Experimenting with food in your spare time at home is also an invaluable experience.

CATERING THE FUTURE

If you're interested in catering, the most lucrative path is to be self-employed. Working from your kitchen and using store-bought supplies to prepare meals for small events means your overhead costs are low. As you gain experience and clients, you may find yourself in a position to expand your business, perhaps renting out a kitchen and working with suppliers. However, as with other small businesses, the income gained from catering is entirely dependent on identifying clients. If your marketing is ineffective and doesn't generate enough clients, the business will never get off the ground.

If you decide to work for a catering company, the pay depends on what services you are personally performing. The goal is to work your way up to becoming a key member of a hotel or private catering team.

Catering, alongside other positions in the food service industry, is a steadily growing field. There are many ways to break into the catering business, though it can be competitive, as there are only so many clients available at any given time. There are always jobs available with established businesses, or you can take a risk and create your own opportunity by branching out alone. If you come up with an interesting variation on the general field of catering—or just provide consistently great service and tasty food—the future in this line of work can be very bright.

CHAPTER 6

WHEN FOOD GETS PERSONAL

The modern world is undeniably busy. From swamped businesspeople to panicking parents, there are a lot of people who simply don't have time to get in front of the stove and prepare meals. On top of that, think of all the clueless cooks out there—some people don't have the skill to make the food they'd like to eat. What can these people do? For those with enough money, it's possible to hire a personal chef.

As the title implies, these cooks don't work in a restaurant, instead they are getting paid by a single customer (or group of clients) to cook personalized meals in their home. Because personal chefs don't have the security of an entire restaurant behind them, they have to be true masters of their craft. Most successful personal chefs are classically trained and have strong organizational and interpersonal skills. Most chefs don't step out of the kitchen often—but a personal chef *only* works in full view of their customers. This can be highly stressful, but the job is also very rewarding for those who thrive on small-scale interactions.

PUTTING YOUR TOUCH ON IT

What distinguishes being a personal chef from many other careers in the food industry is that they are their own bosses. Technically, personal chefs are small business owners, meaning they can set their own hours, rates of pay, and clientele.

Becoming an executive chef in a restaurant takes talent, luck, and years of work experience. Until they reach that point, many chefs spend a good deal of time assisting head chefs, who ultimately decide which dishes will be served. Starting your own business puts you in charge of everything, including every foodie's dream: the chance to develop your own unique creations, menus, and identity.

Personal chefs prepare food based on their clients' needs and preferences. One family may want comfort foods, like meatloaf or pork chops, while a health-conscious couple may request a week's worth of low-calorie vegetarian meals. Another special request may be to develop meals around a person's dietary restrictions or allergies. For example, if a child is lactose intolerant, a personal chef needs to adjust their menu accordingly. An important quality for a personal chef is versatility: with a broad knowledge of flavors, food preparation techniques, and menu planning, personal chefs can increase their client base—and ability to make money—significantly.

A personal chef must be able to give their clients what they want, which typically means working out menus and budgets well before the cooking happens.

Personal chefs do far more than just cook. They must follow a strict food budget and shop for the best and freshest ingredients, all while keeping their clients' preferences and culinary identity in mind. This could mean simultaneously shopping for several different families that all have different budgets, menus, and quantities of food to receive. To keep all this straight, organizational skills are extremely important.

If you prepare your clients' meals in advance, make sure you use proper food storage and safety techniques.

The majority of personal chefs do not decide to "wing it" when they arrive at their clients' houses—they come fully prepared with preplanned menus. Personal chefs usually prepare meals at the beginning of the week and leave the meals in the refrigerator or freezer to be completed later. Though this may sound easy, knowledge of food storage and advance prep is key. Certain foods may need to be kept at a lower temperature than others, and storing them in the same refrigerator could ruin those meals.

The chance to have close working relationships—and possibly friendships—with one's clients is a great bonus in this line of work. Personal chefs often see their clients frequently and develop strong relationships with the people who eat and enjoy their food. This is both personally rewarding and helpful for self-improvement and networking. Some personal chefs may even live part-time in the house of the family whose food they prepare. In these cases, they are referred to as private chefs.

Title aside, becoming a personal or private chef is a great option for an independent, self-driven person who loves to cook and share food with people he or she cares about. If you aren't a fan of dealing with the same people several times a week—possibly for years—then this job may not be for you.

PERSONAL QUALIFICATIONS

To make it as a personal chef, you must be experienced in the art of cooking and have a thorough knowledge of food preparation, food storage, and nutritional planning. All of these skills will be credentials that get your foot in the door for new clients. Keeping your customers is a different story—that's where people skills come in. Restaurants have sturdy doors to separate the cooking staff from the clientele, and the two rarely collide. There is no barrier for personal chefs and their customers. Being friendly and flexible is a must.

People will only want to hire a well-qualified personal chef, so experience and training are absolute necessities.

It is possible to become a personal chef without formal training. This is especially true outside of major culinary hubs, like New York City, where there may be a shortage of personal chefs. Though there are some success stories of people leaving their office jobs and starting up a booming personal chef enterprise, there are many more stories of

people working as personal chefs only part-time. Imagine someone with a secure job at a bank that provides a steady paycheck, but who also loves cooking on the weekends. Instead of inviting friends and family over, maybe they reach out to get clients and start using their weekend time to prepare meals for them. Voilà: they have just become a part-time personal chef, making a little extra money and getting to explore their culinary talents with little risk.

Though making it as a self-taught chef is possible, many personal chefs are classically trained. They often come to the job having studied at professional culinary schools, which gives them a strong foundation for starting a business. Many personal chefs start cooking in restaurant or hotel kitchens before setting out to become self-employed entrepreneurs. Experience is key regardless of the path you take, since your clients will only choose to work with you if you have a proven ability to deliver a great product consistently.

If you decide you're ready to strike out on your own as a personal chef, it may be a good idea to join a professional association to help you find work in your field and meet people who have experience with the position. Associations like these commonly offer certification programs, which can be a big résumé booster. The field is very competitive, and having some credentials will assist you in interviews with potential clients.

THE FUTURE IN YOUR HANDS

There are two major factors to consider when thinking about a personal chef's income: time invested and number of clients served. Many personal chefs are paid hourly, while others are paid a flat rate based on the number and frequency of meals they provide.

Location will also have a major influence on a personal chef's income. For example, a successful personal chef in New York City will make more than a personal chef in Kansas City, simply because of the difference in the cost of living. It's important to note that while major metropolitan areas will offer a higher ceiling of potential pay, it will likely be easier to find employment in a smaller city, as highly populated areas are naturally more competitive.

Personal chefs are largely in control of their own destiny, and, as such, they have the opportunity to make as much money as they want, as long as there is demand for their services and they can accumulate happy customers. People are getting busier and busier all the time. The number of families with two working parents is growing. People are putting in long hours on the job, and some simply view cooking as a chore after a long day of hard work. The growing demand for personal chefs reflects this.

Being able to provide families with a nutritious and delicious meal after a hard day is a skill that is both appreciated and sought after. Decades ago, many people would have laughed at the thought of paying someone else to cook them dinner at home. Today's busy society is different. Now is a great time to pursue a career as a personal chef, as long as you prepare yourself for the demands of this unique career.

CHAPTER 7

IT'S TIME TO BAKE

As a basic food known and used the world over, bread has long been the subject of human inspiration. Ever heard the phrase "bread and butter"? It refers to something that's fundamentally important—just like bread.

Bakers are the professionals who have perfected the art of breadmaking over the years—and they didn't stop there. Bakers are also responsible for creating cookies, cakes, muffins, and so much more. Using the essentials—eggs, flour, sugar, butter—they bring both sweet and savory products to the world at large.

NOT A PIECE OF CAKE

Bakers are professionals who spend their days—and sometimes nights—making delicious baked goods for customers to enjoy. Working in a bakery or bakeshop, bakers do much more than open a box of cake mix and go to work. The key phrase for most

Bakers cover a lot of ground in their kitchens—their creations can range from sweet desserts to hearty breads.

bakers is "from scratch." This means that good bakers have come up with their own perfect combinations of ingredients that are needed to produce a great birthday cake or several mouthwatering loaves of bread. They don't rely on prepackaged products to prepare their food—and the taste proves it!

Bakers must have a strong eye for detail because they spend much of their time following recipes and weighing, measuring, and mixing ingredients. Believe it or not, a lot of baking comes down to chemistry. That may sound a little intimidating, but bakers don't need a degree in science to be successful. They just need a basic understanding of how and why baking ingredients react with each other. Bakers differentiate themselves by devising brand-new recipes with unique ingredients (within reason) or by adding a special twist to a common recipe. The personal touches a baker adds to their products is what keeps people coming back to that specific bakery.

Bakers spend a lot of time around huge ovens that are extremely hot, so safety is a major concern in this career. Every time bakers open an oven to put in or take out their creations, they risk serious burns or a flash of heat in the face. Bakers need to be mindful of their backs and legs as well. The large bags of flour, sugar, and cornmeal they need for cooking are heavy. Combined with the stress of standing on one's feet for 10 to 12 hours a day, bakers run the risk of straining their backs from lifting and

The ratio of one ingredient to another can make or break any baked good.

stooping often. It's a lot harder than whipping up a batch of cookies at home.

This is also not the career for late sleepers. Many bakeries that open to the public bright and early in the morning have already had their ovens working for hours. The early bird catches the worm—and in the case of bakers, they need to be up long before everyone else if they want to get ready for the morning rush. In addition to the early hours, most bakeries have staff stay after the doors close in the evening to help prepare the next day's tasty treats.

Just as in restaurants, there are many kinds of work environments for bakers. Some bakers work in independent bakeshops serving local communities on a small scale. There's more creative freedom in this environment since you'll likely be the only baker or part of a small team of specialists. There are also job opportunities at chain stores that have a presence around the country. Working in this environment, bakers have to follow a predetermined recipe book, much like a cook. Deviating from these recipes can cost you your job since the company has formulated its recipes to satisfy the public and maintain the brand identity it wants to convey. Finally, bakers also have the option of working for large-scale bakeries in grocery stores or factories. The bakers in these places turn out large volumes of baked products, rather than a smaller quantity of carefully crafted goods.

Where you work determines the day-to-day job responsibilities. If you work for a large-scale operation, you'll be one of many, with less responsibility; if you work for a local bakery, everything may rest on your shoulders. Choosing between these options can be difficult. It all depends on where you'd feel most comfortable.

LEAVENING YOUR SKILLS

Just as with many jobs in the food industry, a college degree isn't necessary to become a baker— but experience is. Working as an apprentice is the best way to start a career in baking. An apprentice is a person who works under the supervision of a seasoned professional while they learn the basics of a job. At the beginning of your apprenticeship, you may be asked to fetch ingredients or perform only the most basic tasks while watching and learning. As

Every baker has to start somewhere—and learning from someone with real experience will help you on your path to success.

you gain experience, you may be allowed to try your hand at some of the easier techniques. In the case of professional baking, observing an experienced baker will allow you to see how to accurately execute a variety of baked goods.

Apprenticeships are highly desirable because you often get paid to learn from the best. However, they're not readily available, so competition is tough. It's a good idea to get a head start on the competition by searching for one as early as possible. Chances are, you won't be decorating cakes when you start; most bakery helpers spend their hours on the job cleaning pots, rolling pins, and mixing bowls. If landing an apprenticeship is impossible, you may also begin by working a regular part-time job at your local bakery or grocery store. These places are typically willing to take on students and young adults, especially if it can spark a lifelong interest in baking.

There are two other great places to seek experience. If you attend a vocational high school, you may be able to take a baking course. This kind of class will teach you the basics of the craft and expose you to specialized baking equipment. Take advantage of this option if it's available to you: it can give you insight into the profession and provide networking opportunities if you choose to pursue a career in baking.

The last option is simple: bake at home! Invest a little in cookbooks, watch baking shows, or look for recipes online. It's better to try and fail first in your own kitchen than to make your first attempts in an

Getting hands-on baking experience can be as simple as turning on your oven at home and experimenting with ingredients!

actual bakery. Plus, bakeries are more likely to hire you if you can demonstrate some practiced skills. A delicious plate of cookies couldn't hurt either!

PROSPECTS FOR BAKERS

The highest-paid retail bakers belong to professional unions. Unfortunately, not every business that employs bakers is unionized. You'll usually find unionized bakers in grocery stores, factories, and larger establishments. Independent bakeshops and small-scale operations aren't likely to have unionized workers, as the cost is simply too high.

Most bakers are paid hourly, and the pay rate matches their experience. Expect to make minimum wage as an apprentice. Moving up from there, bakers will see pay increases based on how long they've been with the company and how talented they prove to be. Note that some bakers choose to specialize in one particular area, such as cake decorating. A skilled specialist can command the highest pay rate since they have a highly sought-after skill. Bakers in this category are referred to as artisans. Pastry chefs also fall into this category.

The Bureau of Labor Statistics reports that prospects for aspiring bakers are quite good, with an expected 6 percent growth between 2018 and 2028. From local hotspots to chain grocery stores with consistent quality, there will always be a need for passionate, experienced bakers working the ovens all across the world.

CHAPTER 8

CO-OPS: A NEW GROCERY STORE

Most communities in the United States have several large grocery stores, with some or all of them likely being large nationwide chains. These supermarkets offer a wide variety of items—including food, medicine, beauty products, and more—that are available year-round for affordable prices. Many families do most or all of their shopping at establishments like this.

There has been an upward trend, however, in the emergence of stores called food cooperatives (co-ops), which are essentially small grocery stores that are collectively owned by their members. For a small fee, people who live near a co-op are able to purchase shares in the store—making them co-owners with any of their neighbors who also purchase shares. Co-ops generally offer a smaller variety of goods than traditional grocery stores, but the quality is often much higher. These establishments serve as a fresher, healthier alternative for buying food compared to large chains, and their employees are people who are passionate about the food products they're selling.

MAKING MONEY AT A NONPROFIT

The jobs at a food co-op are similar to the jobs found at a traditional supermarket or large food store. For example, most co-ops have department managers and buyers. In some cases, a manager also does the purchasing for their department, whether it's

If you volunteer at a co-op, you'll get the chance to see what its daily operations are like.

produce, beauty aids, or baked goods. A good buyer/ manager needs to know what is and isn't in stock. They also need to know when the out-of-stock items will be available again from the supplier. Department managers generally report to a general manager. This individual is responsible for the day-to-day operation of the co-op, which can include processing payroll, reading reports, and addressing employee concerns.

The best way to get your foot in the door at a food co-op is to register as a volunteer or join. Most co-ops require that their members volunteer before they can enjoy the benefits of membership. By working as a co-op volunteer, you have the opportunity to become familiar with the daily routine of keeping the store up and running. This exposure will make obtaining a paid position easier since the staff will know you already and see that you are dedicated to their cause. You'll also have real hands-on experience you can apply to a paid position.

Most co-op employees spend their fair share of time working in lower-level positions before graduating to better-paying jobs. Demonstrating a knack for getting things done quickly and correctly can accelerate this process. Additionally, if the co-op experiences a lot of growth and increased revenue, anyone contributing to its success will likely be rewarded.

People enjoy working at co-ops because of the community spirit and teamwork found there. Everybody is working for a common cause, and this creates a friendly and satisfying atmosphere. Since

CO-OP HISTORY

The idea of the food cooperative was first documented in the 19th century in the little town of Rochdale, England. A small group of individuals ran a cooperative market as a way to reduce the burden of everyone having to provide everything they needed on their own. The Rochdale Pioneers, as they were called, focused on principles of sharing and community over independent self-sufficiency.

The co-op idea eventually found its way to the United States. The number of food cooperatives exploded between the years of 1969 and 1979, with the total reaching nearly 10,000 markets. Food co-ops provided an organic,

There has never been a stronger push for organic food options than in the late 2010s, and grocery stores and co-ops are answering the call to provide them.

anticorporate alternative to traditional chain stores. In other words, cooperatives fit right in with the mind-set of many people in 1970s America.

The number of food co-ops began to dwindle after the heyday of the 1970s, but in the 2010s, they have slowly started to emerge again. The cooperative idea has also had a great influence on many modern food stores. Today, there are a number of popular all-organic grocery stores, and even global chains have begun making an effort to carry organic and locally sourced food.

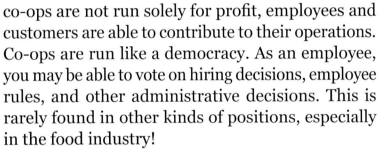

co-ops are not run solely for profit, employees and customers are able to contribute to their operations. Co-ops are run like a democracy. As an employee, you may be able to vote on hiring decisions, employee rules, and other administrative decisions. This is rarely found in other kinds of positions, especially in the food industry!

One potential drawback to working in a food co-op is that the focus is not on generating revenue. As such, wages are sometimes less than in some other food-related jobs—though if your local co-op is highly successful, you may find your compensation package to be better than at a traditional grocery store. In either case, the democratic principles on which a co-op is based—coupled with the fair and friendly environment—are a welcome change for many people.

CO-OP QUALITIES

The best way to get started at a food co-op is to simply walk in and talk to the people who work there. They will likely be more than willing to give you an overview of the co-op and answer any questions you may have. After all, these establishments thrive on community involvement, so they are always looking for ways to bring new people into the fold.

Before committing to a job or signing up for volunteer hours, it may be a good idea to join the co-op as a member and see if you enjoy the general environment. If the fee is too expensive, ask if you can work for free in exchange for a temporary membership or see if they have any special rates for those with lower incomes or students. Training—as with many jobs in food markets—is commonly accomplished through hands-on work and on-the-job experience.

WHAT TO LOOK FORWARD TO

Pay rates for employees of a co-op are highly varied and are affected by position, location, and membership. Also, a larger, more established food co-op is more likely to pay a higher wage than a brand-new one. The manager of a co-op will earn a higher salary than buyers or cashiers, as they have likely been there a long time or had years of experience at other co-ops or grocery stores. Again, some food co-ops may pay employees less than other food stores, simply because the focus of the business is not generating profits. Some, however, might pay more than a regular grocery store.

Consumers are concerned about food integrity now more than ever. They need places that provide local, sustainable, and safe food, and co-ops answer this desire. Co-ops need employees and volunteers to help further their mission, so finding a job in one shouldn't be difficult if you're committed to working in that environment.

CHAPTER 9

WRITING ABOUT EATING

Not everyone has the passion for cooking that's required to achieve success in the kitchen—instead, maybe you have a passion for eating. When coupled with a talent for writing, this passion can turn into one of the most enviable positions in the entire food industry: food critic.

Critics, or reviewers, are people who are paid to write fair, honest, and thoughtful reviews of restaurants and food. These critiques are typically published in magazines, newspapers, or online publications. Imagine getting paid by a publisher to visit restaurants, eat food, and tell people about the experience. It sounds like—and is—the dream job for many people. However, the profession comes with its own set of challenges and requirements.

FARM TO . . . PAGE?

Food critics who want to be successful must have two important qualities: a refined palate and strong writing ability. Unlike in many food-related professions, your taste buds are probably the less important of these skills. People don't want to read reviews that describe a meal as just "good" or "OK"; food critics are expected to provide thoughtful, insightful, and well-thought-out accounts of their overall dining experience with every review. A mastery of language is worth its weight in gold. Penning a sentence such as, "The chicken arrived shriveled and tough, its meat unyielding to my fork and knife," is much more interesting than simply writing, "The chicken was dry."

If you want to review food, you'll probably want to take notes as you eat so you don't forget anything about the meal.

In addition to writing about the quality of the food itself, food critics often report on the restaurant's service, ambiance, and décor since going to a restaurant involves more than just what's on the plate. What separates a decent food critic from a great food critic is the ability to make readers feel as though they're experiencing everything firsthand. Critics achieve this immersion by not skimping on small details. They might describe how the food was artfully plated or mention something noteworthy about the service they received. Maybe the food is great, but the waiter accidentally spills a drink all over a reviewer's new shirt. The review will need to weigh the positive and negative aspects of each restaurant to determine whether the review will be favorable or not.

As an aspiring food critic, you'll want to arm yourself with a deep understanding of food and the way it's prepared. A degree from a culinary school isn't required, but attending a few courses may help. Some food critics were once chefs or cooks themselves. Knowing how food is prepared gives food critics a better idea of how a meal should taste, including the ability to identify what's good and bad about certain dishes. Plus, having some experience in restaurant kitchens makes you credible in the eyes of readers. They're more likely to trust your opinion if you have more knowledge on the subject than they do.

As enticing as it sounds to be paid to write about food, this profession is not for the faint of heart (or stomach). Good critics must be able to eat adventurously—and often. They may eat a standard steak-and-potatoes meal at one restaurant and then fish eggs at another. A food critic may need to make multiple trips to the same eatery if its menu goes through frequent changes. If you're a picky eater, this definitely isn't the right field for you.

Food critics must also consider their weight as they go from restaurant to restaurant. A job that involves eating, eating, and more eating directly affects the waistline. Food critics have to be careful

Both print and broadcast news outlets often put out food review columns or segments to keep their customers informed about local eateries.

to not let their job compromise their overall health. If you choose to go into this profession, you may want to invest in both a computer and running sneakers!

With all that in mind, if you're still interested in food criticism, where can you find work? Local news shows, radio programs, newspapers, and magazines are the most common employers. The average critic with a secure position reviews one or two restaurants each week. This may or may not provide a livable salary. Therefore, many critics review food for several different publications or have another job on days they're not writing about restaurants.

One final word: it's important to be honest and fair at all times. The word "critic" doesn't mean that the writing always has to be negative. If the food is not very good, a wise critic might provide constructive criticism or give suggestions on how to improve a certain meal or restaurant.

A RECIPE FOR WORD SALAD

There is no such thing as a degree in food criticism. This is great news for the person who finds the idea of college unappealing. However, strong writing skills are a must, so some continuing education is probably necessary.

To enter this line of work, work on your writing and knowledge of food consistently. Joining your school's newspaper or writing club is a great way to start building experience in putting pen to paper (or fingers to keyboard). These clubs may allow you to write local restaurant reviews for them. For something a little less formal, you can check out various restaurant and business review websites, such as Yelp. These sites give regular people the opportunity to write about a restaurant as amateur critics. This could be a great way to try your hand at reviewing food since other users will often tell you if they find your comments helpful.

Another avenue is to volunteer part-time at a local newspaper or television show that reviews food regularly. Food critics usually write for the Weekend or Lifestyles sections of newspapers. Try writing a few sample reviews on your own and see what a local newspaper or magazine editor thinks. This is a good way to get solid and honest feedback on your writing while also introducing yourself to potential employers.

If none of these opportunities are open to you, browse through cookbooks and books on food. Subscribe to a food magazine and read its reviews, or watch food shows on TV. The key is to get involved in this industry early and learn as much as you can. You may want to start cooking exotic foods at home or experimenting with trying adventurous meals at nearby restaurants. Try as many different types of food as possible to expand your palate. The more you know about food, the more you can write about food.

Remember: if people like their jobs, they probably like to talk about them. Make connections at a local television station or newspaper and ask if you can meet with a food critic. Contact a food critic via the

Big cities like Toronto, Canada, offer the best opportunities—but also the toughest competition—for aspiring food critics.

internet and ask them questions about their job. The critic may know about employment opportunities or may be able to advise you on how to get started.

FORWARD-LOOKING REVIEW

Food critics' salaries differ, and one large factor is the publisher of their reviews. A critic whose work is placed in a monthly national magazine is likely making more money than someone who writes for the local newspaper. Food critics are writers first, and they can be paid per word or per article. The rate and method of pay is determined by the individual publication. Contact various magazines or papers to see what each one offers food writers.

Competition is very tough in this profession—who wouldn't want to eat great food and get paid to write about it? More food critics can be found in areas with larger populations because there are more publications that employ them. A small city may have only one newspaper, but large cities like Los Angeles, Toronto, or Chicago may have three or four daily publications. Regardless, the key is to decide early on that you want to be a food critic and then devote your time to getting there.

CHAPTER 10

EATING YOUR ART

F ood is art. For those passionate about cooking, there is no doubt in their minds that this statement is true. For common people, however, food doesn't look like art—unless a stylist has gotten ahold of it. Food styling is an important job in the industry, and it exists at the intersection of cooking, advertising, and design. Most stylists know how to cook, how to plate food, and, most importantly, how to make it look visually stunning. Alongside food photographers, these skilled professionals are responsible for bringing the language and artistry of the kitchen into the world for all to see.

DOING IT WITH STYLE

First and foremost, food stylists are cooks who are in charge of the food items that are involved in a food photography shoot. They obtain ingredients, cook them, and ensure that the prepared food remains ready to be photographed. This often means

Food photography is more than just taking pictures for social media—it's a serious production!

maintaining a uniform look throughout a busy day of shooting and reshooting.

Preparing food for its time in the spotlight requires many different talents. These skills fall somewhere between art and science. Food stylists need to thoroughly understand the properties of the foods they cook. They must know things such as how far in advance an item can be made or if something will lose its color over time. This is especially important when working with foods that will melt or spoil if not refrigerated.

The conditions during photo shoots can be tough on food. Imagine what a pint of ice cream looks like after spending hours under the hot glare of bright lights! To make sure all the food on set is looking its best, food stylists may have to chemically alter the food they've prepared. This is where science and art start to mix in a way that's not normally seen in a kitchen. A basic knowledge of chemistry can help a stylist out; a few shakes of salt or a drop or two of a preserving liquid can help extend a food's life without affecting its appearance.

Food stylists are responsible for tasks such as plating food or arranging all of a dish's components in a visually attractive way. The photographers then capture these arrangements and turn them into the mouthwatering images we see all around us. Think about all the images you see every day in food magazines or restaurant menus—they make you hungry for a reason. Food stylists and photographers are paid to turn the average dinner plate into an attractive work of art.

Food stylists and photographers often report to clients directly. A typical customer could be a local restaurant, food blog, newspaper, or magazine. Some publications employ a small team of food stylists and photographers to cover different categories of food or different spreads they want to produce.

Whether you're employed by a large or small business—or even if you freelance—clients commonly want their food to look like it has just been freshly

THE RIGHT TOOLS FOR THE JOB

Perhaps the most important quality for a food stylist is the ability to adapt on the fly. Since the entire shoot depends on them, flexibility is key. Many stylists carry an ordinary fishing tackle box filled with supplies—but the contents are a far cry from what a fisherman needs. Interestingly, few of the items in the tool kit have anything to do with food. Here are some items a food stylist typically keeps on hand:

- Nonfood supplies, including paper towels, tweezers, toothpicks, cotton swabs, razor blades, oil, paintbrushes, electric mixer, blowtorch, spray bottle, hot plate, ice chest or cooler, cutting board, knives, sponges, ice cream scoop, measuring spoons and cups, glue, plastic ice cubes, paint stripper, pins, glycerin, and erasers.
- Food supplies, including pepper, instant potatoes, jam, jelly, marmalade, flour, rice, maple syrup, parsley, salt, cinnamon, oregano, and kitchen bouquet (a sauce for browning and seasoning).

prepared, even if it has been sitting around for hours. This provides an appealing image to customers, which ultimately brings in business. These demands mean that no food stylist travels too far without a kit of ingredients, chemicals, and tools to handle any sticky situation.

In addition to being experts in food, stylists must be able to work effectively as members of a team. They work with photographers, art directors, and the client who is paying for the featured food. Some stylists may have assistants to help clean the cooking items or carry other equipment.

Food stylists are professionals with many skills, and being a good team player is one of the most important.

TAKING YOUR SHOTS

If you're interested in trying your hand at styling food, experience in cooking and baking is an essential requirement. This experience can come from different sources. Some food stylists have spent time as personal chefs or restaurant cooks, while others have attended culinary schools. Most culinary or cooking schools offer courses in food styling, but not full degrees in it. This is an advantage if you want to get started without a degree.

Another important step toward working with food as art is apprenticing. Many hopeful food stylists seek employment under the instruction of seasoned veterans. After that, they can become apprentices. Cooking skills are important for stylists (less so for photographers), but the most important aspect of these professions is a keen eye for presentation. One way to become proficient as either a stylist or a photographer is to watch someone perform in their actual work environment. This will give you a clear sense of what it takes to be successful.

Working for a veteran stylist or photographer will give you hands-on experience and help you develop a portfolio of work, which you'll need to show potential clients or employers when you strike out on your own. Learning all of the ins and outs of the profession can be time consuming, so be patient and learn as you go.

PHOTOGRAPHING THE FUTURE

As with other food-related careers, the income of a food photographer or stylist is highly dependent on location. There's more work to be found in larger cities, but also much more competition. One reason for the greater availability of work in large cities is that many magazine publishers and television and movie companies are based in more densely populated areas, like New York or Los Angeles.

People see the work of food stylists every time they turn on the TV or open a newspaper, so it's important that the food look as good as possible!

Food stylists in big cities are likely to make more money than professionals in smaller locales. Assistant salaries are far lower than those of full-fledged stylists or photographers, but this pay rate varies by employer.

More and more culinary schools are adding food styling to the courses they offer, which is a sign that these positions are in demand. Because advertising and presenting food products will never go out of style, developing the artistic and culinary skills necessary to succeed in this career will likely pay dividends for years.

A career is food photography is a little different because it's common to obtain a degree in photography. This amount of formal training is not an absolute necessity, however. If you're interested in photography, you should put together a portfolio of your work. Even if it's not all focused on food, you can present this to a potential client as proof of your abilities behind the lens.

GLOSSARY

ambiance The character and atmosphere of a particular setting, such as a restaurant or hotel.

apprentice A person who learns a trade from a skilled employer.

celebrity chefs Experienced cooks who have risen to the top of the food industry based on their talent and personality.

clientele The customers of a business, such as a bar, shop, or restaurant.

cooperative A farm, business, or other organization that is owned and run jointly by its members.

cost of living A general idea of how much it costs to live in a certain area; includes housing, food, and transportation costs.

critiques Detailed assessments of something.

culinary Related to the profession of cooking.

customer service Assistance and courtesy given to customers.

entry-level Suitable for workers who are just starting out in the workforce.

food blog An online site with posts about food, recipes, or restaurants.

foodie A person who is highly interested in food, ingredients, cooking, and food trends.

garde-manger A chef responsible for directly handling and preparing cold food.

lucrative Capable of producing a lot of profit.

palate A person's appreciation for taste and flavor.

portfolio A collection of work samples, photographs, documents, or other items that display a person's professional skills.

repertoire The set of skills that a person has learned and is prepared to demonstrate.

saucier A chef who prepares sauces, soups, stews, and sautéed food.

sauté To cook quickly in a little bit of fat, such as butter or oil; a dish prepared in this manner.

seniority The state of working in a position for longer than someone else.

sous chef A chef who ranks directly under the executive or head chef.

sustainable Describing something that is used in a manner that allows it to be replenished.

turnover The rate at which employees leave a field and are replaced with new hires.

upscale Relating or appealing to wealthy customers; luxurious.

vocational Directed at a specific occupation or set of job skills.

Baking Association of Canada

7895 Tranmere Drive, Suite 212
Mississauga, ON L5S 1V9
Canada
(888) 674-2253
Website: https://www.baking.ca/index.aspx
Facebook: @bakeryhowcase
This trade organization represents bakers and bakery owners
from across Canada. It hosts events for professionals and helps
spread information and news about the industry.

National Restaurant Association

2055 L Street NW, Suite 700
Washington, DC 20036
Website: https://restaurant.org/Home
Facebook, Instagram, and Twitter:
@WeRRestaurants
This professional organization, with more than
40,000 members, offers training and certification programs
for both existing restaurateurs and those hoping to break
into the industry.

Occupational Safety and Health Administration (OSHA)

200 Constitution Avenue NW
Washington, DC 20210
(800) 321-6742
Website: https://www.osha.gov
Facebook: @departmentoflabor
Instagram: @usdol
Twitter: @OSHA_DOL

A division within the U.S. Department of Labor, OSHA regulates workplace safety across the country—a particular concern within the food industry. Its website features information about your rights and responsibilities as an employee or an employer.

Restaurant Facility Management Association (RFMA)

2801 Network Boulevard, Suite 100
Frisco, TX 75034
(972) 805-0905
Website: https://www.rfmaonline.com
Facebook: @RFMAonline
Twitter: @RFMA
There are many people who help restaurants run smoothly besides cooks and chefs, and the RFMA is a vocational organization committed to serving those people. The association offers training, education, and information for anyone who wants to join—or is already in—the restaurant business.

Restaurants Canada

1155 Queen Street West
Toronto, ON M6J 1J4
Canada
(416) 923-1450
Website: https://www.restaurantscanada.org
Facebook and Instagram: @RestaurantsCanada
Twitter: @RestaurantsCA
Representing restaurants and food service businesses across Canada, this organization's aim is to help those working in the industry succeed. Its website offers background information and breaking news related to the field of food.

Society for Hospitality and Foodservice Management (SHFM)

326 East Main Street

Louisville, KY 40202

(502) 574-9931

Website: https://www.shfm-online.org

Facebook: @foodservicemanagement

Instagram: @shfmgmt

Twitter: @FoodserviceMgmt

Dedicated to serving the needs of managers in the restaurant and hospitality industries, SHFM is an invaluable resource for anyone looking to advance in these fields. Becoming a member comes with a wide variety of perks, including easy access to networking opportunities within the industry.

FOR FURTHER READING

Dixon, Rachel. *Food and Cooking*. Belrose, Australia: Redback Publishing, 2018.

Gluckstern, Rachel. *Working in Restaurants and Catering*. New York, NY: Rosen YA, 2019.

Marlowe, Christie, and Andrew Morkes. *Chef: A Culinary Artist*. Philadelphia, PA: Mason Crest, 2020.

Nagle, Jeanne. *Gordon Ramsay*. New York, NY: Enslow Publishing, 2016.

Parks, Peggy J. *Careers in the Culinary Arts*. San Diego, CA: ReferencePoint Press, 2020.

Smythe, Katie. *Cooking Is Science*. New York, NY: Rosen Publishing, 2016.

Stoltman, Joan. *Cooking Great Cuisine with a Chef*. New York, NY: Gareth Stevens Publishing, 2019.

Storey, Rita. *How to Make Money from Cooking and Baking*. London, UK: Franklin Watts, 2017.

Twiddy, Robin. *Cooking & Eating*. King's Lynn, UK: Booklife Publishing, 2019.

INDEX

A

ambiance, 80
apprentice, 37–38, 67, 68, 70, 91

B

bakers, 46, 62, 64–66, 67, 68–69
  prospects for, 69–70
  unions and, 69–70
bakery, 62, 64, 65–66, 68–69
budget, 20, 37, 55
Bureau of Labor Statistics, 16, 25, 34, 44, 70
buyer, 72–73, 76

C

catering, 45–47, 48, 49, 50–52
celebrity chefs, 4–5, 35
chef
  becoming a, 5, 41–42, 49
  and catering, 46
  celebrity, 4–5, 35
  and food critics, 80
  head, 6, 35, 37–39, 42, 45, 54
  job security of, 42–44
  life of a, 41
  pastry, 39–40, 70
  personal, 53, 43, 55, 56, 57, 58–59, 60–61, 90
  private, 49, 57
  salaries for, 43–44
  self-taught, 59
  sous chef, 37–39
  successful, 4, 35–36, 37
  versus cooks, 26, 28, 30
  working with managers, 20
clientele, 15, 54, 57
competition, 12, 44, 52, 60, 68, 85, 91
cooking shows, 35
cooks, 4, 17, 20, 21, 26, 30, 31, 32, 38–39, 80, 86, 90
  cold foods, 30
  fry, 30
  grill, 30
  institutional, 31
  line, 26, 30, 32, 42, 51

ABOUT THE AUTHOR

Morgan Williams lives in New York with her husband and two corgis, Tate and Isabelle. She enjoys traveling the world to take in different cultures and cuisines. She's gone on adventures in Japan, Peru, and Iran.

CREDITS